AUTHOR

MEADOWS, B.

CLASS

E

TITLE

Lancashire

LANCASHIRE

A portrait in colour

BILL MEADOWS & RON FREETHY

COUNTRYSIDE BOOKS

Other counties in this series include:

BUCKINGHAMSHIRE   LEICESTERSHIRE & RUTLAND
CHESHIRE   LINCOLNSHIRE
DERBYSHIRE   SUFFOLK
DEVON   SURREY
DORSET   SUSSEX
ESSEX   WARWICKSHIRE

First published 2000
© Photographs, Bill Meadows 2000
© Text, Ron Freethy 2000

08395612

COUNTRYSIDE BOOKS
3 CATHERINE ROAD
NEWBURY, BERKSHIRE

To view our complete range of books,
please visit us at
www.countrysidebooks.co.uk

ISBN 1 85306 598 6

The photograph on page 1 shows Lytham St Anne's plaster decoration
and that on page 4 shows rainbow, near Quernmore

Designed by Mon Mohan
Produced through MRM Associates Ltd., Reading
Printed in Singapore

Contents

INTRODUCTION

'I go into Lancashire tomorrow, that part of the country lying beyond the mountains,
towards the western ocean. I go with a kind of dread, and trust in divine providence.'
William Camden (1551–1623)

Just after the end of the war in 1946 my uncle began to drive a lorry based in Blackpool and specialising in the transport of livestock. As a ten year old I began to keep a diary of the travels which I made as a passenger in his cab. So began my interest in the history and natural history of my native county.

I have been making notes about Lancashire ever since. I well remember my anger in 1974 when the politicians realigned the county boundaries. The new county of Cumbria swallowed the Furness District whilst Greater Manchester and Merseyside appropriated many of the grand old cotton towns of Lancashire.

I was therefore delighted to co-operate in the production of this Portrait of Lancashire with people of like minds. My publisher asked me to write about old Lancashire in terms of geographical and not political boundaries. This was a wonderful challenge and the second bonus was to add words to a series of photographs taken by Bill Meadows.

I have had a camera all my working life and I have taken thousands of snapshots to illustrate my writings. Bill Meadows has also had a camera for many years but Bill has developed his photography into an art form.

It has been a pleasure to celebrate his images and as I wrote each section I had the photographs on my desk in front of me. These evoked fresh memories and have inspired me to take an an even closer look at the county which has given me so much pleasure over the years.

Ron Freethy

Bolton

*'In the sky above them a lark was singing his loudest ∨ over the hills which surround
the valley of the river Irwell and which are for the most part green and rolling.'*
Mrs Humphrey Ward, *Robert Ellesmere* (1893).

In the days before Lancashire cotton was crowned king of the textile world, a small village called Bolton-on-the-Moors made a modest living from the handloom weaving of wool and from farming. Before steam the power of water was the energy source which ran freely and abundantly from the healthy and heathery hills.

The bustling town is now very much 'Bolton-in-the-midst-of-Industry' but what character it has. Here are bustling streets, splendid Victorian civic and commercial buildings, an impressive parish church and a host of historic pubs. Pedestrianised areas mean that some of these architectural gems can be enjoyed at leisure.

Wherever you look Bolton evokes reminders of the cotton industry. Opposite the old market cross is a shop once the premises of Richard Arkwright who, before he made his fortune from textile machinery, earned his living as a barber and wig maker. He travelled the hills and dales around Lancashire purchasing the tresses of, what we might call today, 'follicularly endowed young ladies'.

Despite the rapid development of the town during the Industrial Revolution not all of Bolton's medieval history was demolished and two magnificent medieval, half timbered, manor houses remain. Smithills Hall is a museum based around a very impressive and spacious country park which overlooks a backdrop of sweeping moors and is punctuated by a network of pretty streams.

In complete contrast the Hall i'th' Wood museum (*inset*) is now almost – but thankfully not quite – smothered by housing. This architectural gem is a museum celebrating the history of Bolton in general but also of the life of Samuel Crompton in particular.

Young Sam was a very skilful woodworker and in great secrecy he made his spinning mule which revolutionised the textile industry. The Hall i'th' Wood museum, therefore, ought to be a Mecca for all interested in the history of the cotton industry.

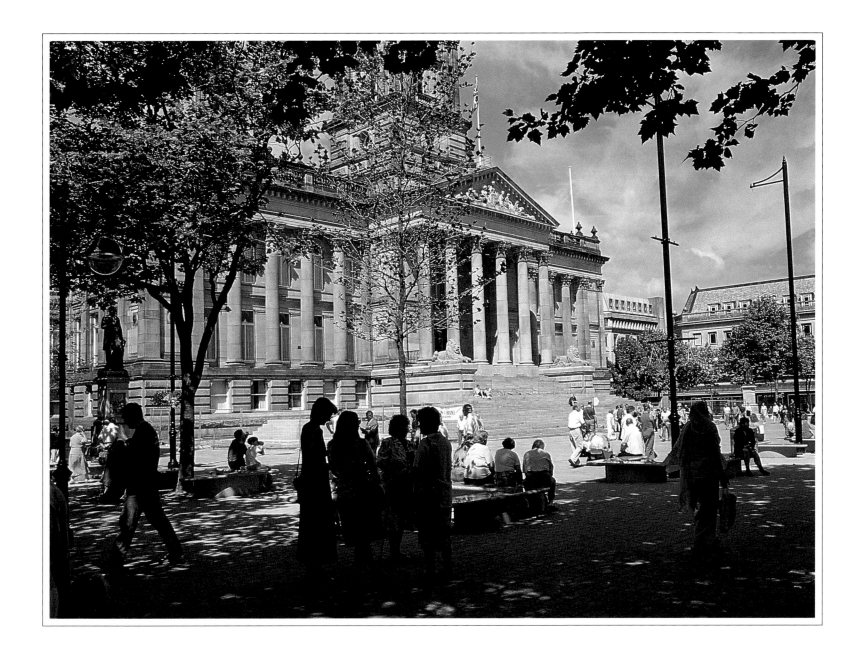

Bolton Market and Football Club

'Bolton, always a progressive town, was the birthplace of great men with great ideas.'
Kathleen Eyre 1971, *The Real Lancashire.*

If you seek to discover the heart and soul of most Lancashire towns the food and football must be major ingredients.

There is nothing I love more than wandering around Bolton's traditional market (*opposite*). You can buy owt from soap to soup, polish to pie and peas, candles to carrots or tea to pigs' trotters. You will be served amid a barrage of Lancashire banter. The streets around the market have the modern touch without losing any of the old world character.

When I look at the new Reebok stadium which is now home to Bolton Wanderers Football Club I find that the team is still known to the older generation as the Trotters.

From a personal point of view I feel the need to apologise to Bolton not once but twice. Football at Burnden Park was a piece of history for those who like to celebrate the founder members of the Football League. I joined the many who objected when the club decided to relocate from Burnden Park in the centre of town to a new stadium at Horwich overlooking the M61 motorway. This has happened and it is a magnificent stadium to look at (*inset*) and surrounded by an impressive shopping complex.

One of the leading lights of the developments at the Reebok was Paul Fletcher. I owe my second apology to Paul. For some years I was schoolmaster in Bolton and I have Paul Fletcher's report in front of me. I wrote: 'Paul would do better to study his biology rather than devoting his short term future to professional football.' He constantly reminds me of this after a career at Bolton and Burnley where he represented England at Under 23 level. Football and the development of impressive modern stadia are still his life.

The Reebok is set overlooking hills around Horwich with rolling moors which serve as catchments for small rivers which in turn feed a chain of reservoirs providing water mainly for Liverpool. On the banks of the reservoir is a replica of Liverpool Castle (the original has long since vanished) built to resemble its ruinous condition in the 17th century.

Salford Quays

'The most well-spoken of all the older Servants in the household of Mrs Nature.'
W.H. Auden (1907–1973), *In Praise of Water.*

The Bridgewater was the first true canal to be built in England and the Manchester Ship Canal was the last. It is a strange twist of fate that both these waterways are now owned by the same company. This is the Manchester Ship Canal Company, a subsidiary of Peel Holdings plc which are owners of the Trafford Centre retail outlet.

The Ship Canal stretches from the River Mersey at Eastham to Manchester, a distance of 36 miles and with five locks. It was begun in 1887 and completed in 1894. It cost a staggering £14.35 million which is impressive even by today's standards.

The MSC, as it is affectionately called, is still a commercially viable waterway but the section around Salford Quays has been sealed off and no longer brings huge ships into the very heart of Trafford Park, which was the first purpose-built Industrial Park in the world.

A great deal of impressive modification, modernisation and innovation has created Salford Quays which is now developing into a major tourist attraction. This will be a centre of attention during the Manchester Commonwealth Games of 2002.

The Lowry Centre (*inset*) will be an important focus for years to come and celebrates the locally born artist made famous for his 'matchstick men' portraits. No one captured the Industrial North better than Lowry and when his paintings are looked at from a distance the matchsticks come alive and look very realistic and nostalgic.

Well into the planning stage is an offshoot of the Imperial War Museum, the construction of which will add yet another dimension to Manchester's already impressive list of art galleries and museums of industrial archaeology.

Around the Quays is a complex of offices, pubs and restaurants set along the old docklands. Great attention has been paid to detail. Old cranes, bollards and protective chains have been neatly and colourfully painted and benches placed in positions which afford panoramic views of an increasingly attractive waterside development.

St Helens

'Tis a concrete of salt and sand or stones.'
Extract from a 16th-century encyclopaedia, describing glass.

Think of St Helens and a Lancastrian will immediately think of Rugby League and glass; a native of St Helens will also add that here was the birth of the canal age in England.

Although it is stated that Britain's first canal was the Bridgewater, actually the Sankey Brook, otherwise known as the St Helens canal, was the very first. It was merely a cut excavated inland from the Mersey estuary but

the stretch, in my opinion, merits the name of canal and it still has colourful boats on it!

The living pulse of the town is the industrial base of Pilkingtons (*opposite*), a company whose name echoes around the world whenever glass production is under discussion. Here are the production bases and also the glass museum (*inset*) which is one of the finest of its type to be found anywhere in the world.

The history of glass making is explained but there are sections devoted to the construction of lighthouses, bullet proof glass, aircraft cockpit canopies (including that of Concorde), and also the hundreds of other uses for this versatile material.

Prior to the coming of the glass industry, St Helens was just a huddle of dwellings set around a chapel from which the town derives its name. During this time the streams, including the Sankey Brook, and also the wells of the developing town were first used and then abused. For a long period during the days of muck and brass, the St Helens canal and the Sankey Brook were like open sewers but with the added problem of a poisonous cocktail shaken and stirred by the chemical industry.

Not far from St Helens, at Widnes, is the Catalyst Museum which graphically tells the story of the chemical industry. All the offensive factories have now gone and the canal is a haven for wildlife with the water clean enough to support fish and birds, such as kingfishers and herons, which prey upon them.

Bury

'Is then no nook of English ground secure from rash assault? ...
William Wordsworth (1770–1850), *On the Projected Kendal and Windermere Railway.*

Whenever I think of Bury I think of black puddings and steam trains, but also I think of a famous prime minister whose family made their brass from cotton but who never forgot his Northern roots.

A day out in this busy town is always a wonderful experience. Travel by steam train from Rawtenstall (*opposite*) along the Irwell Valley to the terminus of the East Lancashire Railway at Bury. From the station it is a short stroll to the grand old market where the 'world championship of black puddings' is held on a weekly basis.

The East Lancashire is a privately operated steam railway company also called the Red Rose Line but to the local folk it is the 'family line'. Many steam railways these days are run purely to attract tourists but the East Lancashire operates a commuter service with reduced fares for local people.

From the track there are panoramic views of the hills above the Irwell and perched on a summit above Ramsbottom is a tower commemorating the life of Sir Robert Peel. The tower was erected in 1852 in memory of Bobby Peel, born in Bury in 1788. This politician instigated the first organised police force, known firstly as 'Peelers' but later as 'Bobbies'.

Sir Robert Peel is also commemorated by a statue set in the centre of Bury (*inset*). He was Prime Minister from 1841 to 1846 and was one of the great influences in the political development of young Queen Victoria.

Peel was also the first to establish the 'penny postal service' in 1840. He was fascinated by communications, no doubt due to his upbringing in cotton country where rail and postal networks were essential for competitive business.

Sir Robert Peel, I am sure, would be delighted with his tower, his statue and the fact that steam trains still trundle along the Irwell Valley!

14

Affetside

'We would be better off without gold than without trees.'
John Evelyn, *Diary* (1664)

Of all the countries in Europe, Britain is the least forested, and of all the English counties, Lancashire has less arboreal cover than most. This is largely because of the ravages caused by the Industrial Revolution which would have horrified the tree-loving diarist, John Evelyn. This contemporary of Pepys provides us with a wonderful insight into the country life of 17th-century England.

At this time Affetside was a more important place than either Bury or Bolton as it is set alongside the old Roman Watling Street. This later became an important coaching route situated at the precise halfway point between London and Edinburgh. Look out also for the remains of the ancient Saxon preaching cross placed in this strategic position (*inset*).

At Affetside is the aptly named Packhorse Inn which provides two sorts of spirit, the less obvious type being in the form of a skull set on top of the bar. This is all that remains of George Whewell who was the executioner of Lord Derby.

In the centre of Bolton is the Derby Column, next to another pub – Ye Old Man and Scythe. A plaque tells us that 'James Stanley seventh Earl of Derby spent the last few hours of his life in the Inn prior to his execution.' The column stands on the spot where George Whewell wielded his axe on 15th October 1651. Thus ended the life of a brave but ruthless Cavalier and the chair in which he sat during his last hours can be seen inside the pub.

Since Whewell's axe Lancashire has seen other axe-men at work and until recently the area around Bolton had lost most of its trees. These days Community Forests are beginning to restore our tree cover and a lot of intelligent planting is going on in and around Bolton as part of the impressive Red Rose Forest Project.

As more trees are planted around the area there are likely to be even more interesting countryside strolls between Bolton and Affetside. I have long thought this stretch of Watling Street along its entire length is as fascinating as anywhere.

Worsley and the Barton Aqueduct

'Rowing down from the river Irwell from Mode Wheel we passed ... the wonderful
Barton aqueduct.
J. Corbett, *The River Irwell* (1868, pub 1907)

These days, although it is sandwiched within the complex of the M62 motorway, Worsley is regarded as a haven of tranquillity amidst the hustle and bustle of 21st-century life. This has not always been the case as here was once a mucky, murky and highly industrialised village dominated by coal mines, offices, workers' cottages, chimneys and a grubby tangle of heavy engineering.

The modern village is now a joy with the old coal yards lying beneath the village green planted in the early 1900s and the only reminder of the industrialised past being the brick chimney, itself now landscaped and with a fountain incorporated. This feature is overlooked by large up-market mock Tudor residences constructed around 1900.

When the canal opened in July 1761 it was the first purpose-built, totally inland waterway and was designed by James Brindley to carry coal from the Duke of Bridgewater's Worsley mines directly into the centre of industrial Manchester.

A towpath leads to the famous Barton Aqueduct which many think is Brindley's masterpiece, but the wonder of the Canal Age which we see today dates to the 1890s when the Manchester Ship Canal was constructed.

Barton Aqueduct is unique in the sense that it carries one canal (the Bridgewater) over another (the Manchester Ship) (*inset*). The moveable section is a 330 ft long steel section. This swings on a central pivot and when the system is in operation huge rubber-coated wedges push firmly together to form watertight joints.

Because the canal emerges from the drainage system of the long closed mines, the iron compounds associated with coal deposits stain the water brown. It is, however, not harmful to wildlife and anglers line the towpath confident of good catches of coarse fish.

The half-timbered building shown in the photograph opposite was once the canal packet house. It was built in the late 18th century and from here packets and passengers were conveyed to and from Manchester in much more comfort than could then be achieved by road.

Without doubt Worsley is an attractive balance between ancient and modern Lancashire. It shows the resilience of nature in the face of old industry.

Rochdale

'Few stories in the industrial life of Lancashire tell of such courage in the face of adversity as the story of the foundation of Co-operation in the county …'
Frank Hird, *Stories and Tales of Old Lancashire* (1911)

There is no doubt that the most famous person produced in Rochdale was the one and only Gracie Fields but there are many others which spring into the minds of those who love Lancashire as much as I do.

There is Edwin Waugh, often called the Lancashire Burns, whilst another dialect poet was Tom Collier who wrote under the pen name of Tim Bobbin. Collier, although he often drank to excess, was still the respected schoolmaster at Rochdale from 1739 until his death in 1786. He also earned his beer money by painting inn signs which accounts for several Lancashire pubs now called 'Tim Bobbin'.

Another Rochdale lad was John Bright, a social reformer, a friend of Queen Victoria and in the days before electronic aids, considered to be the best, or perhaps the loudest, orator of his age.

Around the same time Sir James Kay-Shuttleworth was earning the title of the Father of the English Education System and founder of the first Teachers' Training College. This was in 1840 at St Marks in Chelsea. Sir James Kay married the Shuttleworth heiress and lived with her at Gawthorpe Hall, near Burnley. The family name was then changed to the Kay-Shuttleworths.

A modern day 'Rochdale Rover' is the TV presenter and writer Kieran Prenderville. Born in the town in 1947, Prenderville writes, amongst others, the successful TV series *Ballykissangel*.

Rochdale takes its name from the River Roch which may not be one of the major rivers of the world but spanning it is said to be the world's widest bridge.

Look out also for Toad Lane Museum which marks the spot where Co-operative Trading first began way back in 1844. This enterprise was due to the efforts of the Rochdale Equitable Pioneers Society who were angry at mill owners who had their own shops and forced their workers to buy second rate groceries at inflated prices. This museum (*opposite*) is a wonderful lesson in social history.

There is a magnificent stroll through colourful gardens (*inset*) around Rochdale town centre, with views of the mock Gothic Town Hall which is considered to be the best of its type in Britain.

Wigan

'… the town of Wigan called in Ancient times Wibiggin; of which name I have nothing to say, but that in Lancashire they call buildings and houses Biggins.'
William Camden (1551–1623)

Camden may have nothing to say about Wigan but on behalf of present day tourists there is plenty to celebrate. Here is the home of Wigan Warriors Rugby League Club, one of the most famous in the world. Its new JJB stadium, which it now shares with the soccer club, was completed in 1999 and stands proudly overlooking the River Douglas.

Once regarded as a music hall joke invented by the comedian father of the great George Formby, Wigan Pier (*opposite*) is now one of the most interesting attractions in North West England. The canal water bus links 'The Way We Were' exhibition with the Trencherfield Mill which has one of the largest working steam engines left in the world. Between the two is the Orwell Inn named in celebration of the author George Orwell whose novel *The Road to Wigan Pier* mentions the industrial dereliction in this part of Victorian Lancashire.

When I was a lad it was said that Wigan thrived on the three 'Cs' – coal, cotton and the canal. 'The Way We Were' exhibition housed in the old canal warehouses focuses mainly upon these three aspects.

Despite this industrial veneer Wigan is the oldest borough in Lancashire, has strong Roman connections, and around the town a fierce Civil War battle was fought in the mid 17th century.

Gathurst is close by and is a nostalgic example of an industrial village sliced through by the Leeds to Liverpool

canal and now overlooked by a massive railway bridge and an even more imposing span over the M6 motorway (*inset*).

A fascinating stroll begins at the Navigation Inn which was obviously an important resting place during the heyday of the canal. Still standing are stables where the barge horses were fed, watered, rested up and shod by the resident farrier.

The railway and canal would obviously not be recognised by Camden but he would have known of Gathurst, a hamlet on the banks of the River Douglas which from Wigan still creeps its way quietly towards Ormskirk and Southport.

Southport

'At noon behold a band
Of lovely lasses troop along the sand'

Herbert Collins, *A Victorian Bathing Sunday in Southport* (1940)

The name Southport only dates back to 1792 but it lies within the ancient parish of North Meols which included the villages of Crossens, Marshside and Churchtown, the latter obviously being the religious focus.

Southport is a place of flowers: here are wonderful gardens and at nearby Formby are some of the best and most colourful sand dune systems to be seen in Europe (*inset*).

The Southport flower show has been a pilgrimage for botanists and gardeners since the 1920s. There is no doubt that the many colourful gardens and botanically rich sand dunes, which still grace the town, were the inspiration for the setting up of the flower show rather than the other way round.

The dunes which surround the town today are still visited by eminent botanists but it is not just the rarities which are interesting. Rest harrow grows prolifically and is a mauve coloured and creeping relative of the pea family. The roots of the plant were once dug up, cut up into pieces and shaken up with water. This was then sold as a very refreshing drink under the name of Spanish Water.

Here too are the breeding grounds of the amphibian natterjack toad and the reptilian sand lizard, two of Europe's rarest animals. Both demand the peace and tranquillity of a sand dune system. The toad requires brackish pools to spawn whilst the sand lizard lays its eggs and leaves them to hatch buried in the warmth of the dry sand. These sensitive habitats need to be preserved at all cost and Southport does seem to have achieved the delicate balance between a refined resort and protection for these reptilian, amphibian and botanical rarities.

From its origins Southport was an up-market resort and this is still a place where people love to come shopping. Here are Victorian arcades alongside modern supermarkets. There is also an impressive fairground and an excellent little theatre close to the quiet sand dunes.

Southport certainly has its own unique blend of 'flower power' but its equally unique mix of boutiques and botany will ensure that the resort continues to thrive.

Carr House and Much Hoole

I have watched people stand by the church of St Michael (*opposite*) and on hearing of the discoveries made by the curate Jeremiah Horrocks, who died at the age of only 23, they have said, 'So what! He only discovered the transit of Venus!'

True, but the significance of this is that in 1639 he proved beyond doubt that the planets revolved around the sun and not around the earth. This is why Horrocks was buried in Westminster Abbey and why Isaac Newton regarded him as a genius.

The late Kathleen Eyre recounted his history in this way: 'A young genius and self-taught astronomer from Toxteth came as curate to St Michael's church at Much Hoole built in 1628 as a chapel of ease to Croston. He supplemented his income by tutoring the daughters of the Stone family at nearby Carr House. Jeremiah Horrocks lodged in a room above the porch. By October 1639 he had calculated that the planet Venus would pass between the earth and the sun. This transit had not previously been observed. On Sunday 24th November 1639 and using the most primitive equipment this astronomical first was observed.'

Of all places in Lancashire, therefore, events at Much Hoole and the nearby Carr House (*inset*) could be said to have had more impact on world science than any other spot in England.

Much Hoole and Little Hoole are now separated by the modern A59 road linking Liverpool and Preston but the former settlement is much as it always was. The splendidly proportioned church still dominates a patchwork of cottages and working farms.

Carr House, where Jeremiah Horrocks lodged and worked out his historic calculations, is privately owned but has been gently restored and is the focus of a company specialising in the production and sale of playground furniture.

Churchtown, Southport

'Man's death I tell by doleful knell;
Lightning and thunder I break asunder.
15th-century monastic rhyme, Anon.

The power of church bells has been part of our history since Norman times. William of Normandy passed a law that a certain peal on a bell or bells meant that all the fires in the parish had to be extinguished at eight o'clock at night for safety's sake. This was called the 'couvre feu' or cover fire. This has been altered slightly these days and translates as curfew.

The eight o'clock bell would certainly have been familiar to the villagers around Churchtown. The church is dedicated to St Cuthbert who died in AD 687 and whose jewel-encrusted remains were carted around Lancashire to prevent the treasure being stolen by the Vikings.

There was probably a small chapel at Churchtown long before the Norman Conquest but the first stone structure is dated at 1178. In 1219 St Cuthbert's Eve was designated as a fair day. This was in mid August and the Sunday following, the 20th, became known as Bathing Sunday and folk travelled miles to 'tear off their clothes and frolic in the sea'. This was certainly the origins of Churchtown as a seaside resort and it was many years later that a South-Port was built to accommodate tourists.

What is still now the unspoiled village of Churchtown is another of Lancashire's time warp settlements with pubs, shops, thatched cottages all snuggled around the church (*opposite* and *inset*). On one side of the main road is Meols Hall, one-time home of the Hesketh family. In the 16th and 17th centuries it was a refuge for Catholics persecuted by the fiercely Protestant Tudors. Meols is an old Saxon word meaning a sand hill – an ideal name for this area.

On the opposite side of the road are the famous Botanical Gardens. These are open to the public and include a local history and natural history museum, a boating lake, an aviary and a selection of genteel entertainments and cafes.

St Cuthbert's jewels have long gone but what remains is a sparkling gem in the crown of Lancashire.

Darwen

'I am always sorry when any language is lost because languages are the pedigree of the nations.'
Samuel Johnson (1709–1784)

Standing on the 1,225 ft summit of Darren (Darwen) Moor is a joy, especially when a strong wind is whistling around the solid masonry of the tower. To the folk hereabouts there is just as much pride in their dialect as there is associated with the language of a nation. This is, therefore, Darren Tower and not Darwen!

From a distance the tower looks like a space shuttle about to blast off (*inset*). It was built during the period 1897/98 to commemorate Queen Victoria's Diamond Jubilee. It was constructed at a cost of £800 entirely by public subscription, stands 86 ft and has a viewing platform at the top which is reached by a flight of internal stone steps.

The tower was not only a memorial to the Queen but

a celebration of a great victory won by the local people in 1896. The 'right to roam' is not a modern controversy because the Victorian cotton operatives demanded access to fresh air to function as a 'lung' away from the hard grind and polluted atmosphere of the mills. In 1896, after a tough and bitter struggle, the locals were victorious and allowed to walk over Darwen Moor which had, until then, been a fiercely protected grouse shoot. The tower therefore was, and still is to local people, a celebration of freedom.

The view from the tower and the paths radiating from it are magnificent. The town of Darwen can be seen (*opposite*) with a few of its chimneys remaining from the days of King Cotton. The most famous of all Lancashire's chimneys is the 300 ft monster dominating India Mill. Although this mill is now the base for a number of small industrial units, the chimney is still a well loved monument and was modelled on a Venetian bell tower. This is not only famous because of its role in the history of the cotton industry, but also as a place of pilgrimage for Lancashire's birdwatchers.

Following many years of persecution and pollution the peregrine falcon has, since the 1990s, been making a heartening comeback. One of its early breeding sites has been atop the mill chimney. A good pair of binoculars can reveal the domestic arrangements of the birds whilst their hunting expeditions take them up and over the Darwen Moor. They, like the modern walkers, are 'as free as air'.

Blackburn and Whalley

'Old Pendle, Old Pendle, thou standest alone
'Twixt Burnley and Clitheroe, Whalley and Colne.'
Anon.

A few years ago there was a heated ecclesiastical argument between Blackburn and Whalley with regard to which was the earliest Christian settlement. The Bible tells us, 'Let there be light' but in this case there was too little light and too much heat.

There were certainly two ancient Christian settlements in the area and a longish walk would then have linked the two. Blackburn's early religious identity has been partly suffocated by the events of the Industrial Revolution whilst rural Whalley has retained more of its ancient relics.

Although Blackburn's Cathedral Church of St Mary (*opposite*) was only consecrated in 1926 and restoration has been going on ever since, there has been a religious focus here since AD 596. The church was also mentioned in the Domesday survey.

Blackburn is quite rightly proud of both its religious and textile history, the latter reflected in its excellent museums and civic buildings. I love to visit the market where there are stalls selling black puddings whilst others concentrate on herbal concoctions, especially sarsaparilla. There is now an Asian influence and there are stalls which tempt the palate with the aroma of curry plus other exotic herbs and spices.

Both Blackburn and Whalley are overlooked by Pendle Hill, which has been a place for local people to stroll for generations. Whalley, especially since a bypass was built, has retained all of its medieval charm. Visitors always seem to head for the wonderful abbey ruins (*inset*). The Cistercians built this monastery in 1320 and it was dissolved by Henry VIII in the late 1530s.

Some visitors are so enchanted by the abbey that they miss the even older Norman church which now has many of the abbey's furnishings within it. They also miss the fine collection of Anglo-Saxon crosses in the churchyard and it is these splendid structures which suggest that Whalley was an earlier Christian settlement than Blackburn.

The Leeds to Liverpool Canal

*'The Canal, its barges, horses, and people made the great romance of every day and
the beauty of some of its reaches I can never forget*
John Masefield (1878–1967)

The Leeds to Liverpool canal is a 127/ mile cut slicing through town and countryside between two great counties and linking the Irish and North Seas.

The canal winds its way up into Yorkshire and down into Lancashire with its summit being at Foulridge near Colne (*opposite*). Here is situated one of the wonders of the canal age in Britain – the mile tunnel.

Apart from the tunnel there is a network of reservoirs set around it and built to provide water to slake the thirst of the locks. Operated one way the 75,000 gallons of water needed to work a lock cascades down into Yorkshire and finally reaches the River Humber and the North Sea; operated in the other direction the lock water bubbles and froths its way downhill through Burnley, Blackburn and Wigan and eventually reaches the mighty Mersey and the Irish Sea!

The tunnel is still navigable and these days the entrance at Foulridge is controlled by traffic lights. In the early days, however, it was every barge for itself! The horses did not have to negotiate the darkness of the tunnel and were led up and over the hillside along 'Barge Horse Lane' to rejoin their load at the other end.

In the meantime the barge was operated by man power. Men earned their living powering the barge by pushing with their legs against the roof and walls of the tunnel. These tough guys were known as 'leggers' and hence we have a possible meaning of the term to 'leg it'.

The Foulridge tunnel is now well established along the tourist trail as is the well named Burnley Weavers' Triangle (*inset*). This is set in the arm of a bend along the cut and the area has recently been restored complete with an excellent visitors' centre, a pub and a working stable.

This area graphically proves the boast that Burnley was once the weaving capital of the world. I have lived and worked in and around the town for more years than I care to remember. This means I am biased but to me this is a wonderful old cotton town full of character, history and natural history set amidst panoramic and surprisingly open countryside, in the valley of the River Brun (hence Brun-Lee) and overlooked by the sweeping Pennine hills.

Barrowford

'By thirty hills I hurry down …
And half a hundred bridges'
Alfred Lord Tennyson, *The Brook* (1864)

Although half a hundred bridges is very much an over-statement, Barrowford is one of those industrial villages dominated by neat and wonderful little spans which tell of a majestic history in stone.

Having lived for more than 20 years within walking distance of Barrowford I can see beyond the veneer of the cotton industry and visualise the life of a more rural age.

What locals fancifully call the Roman Bridge (*opposite*) brings back wonderful memories. An even more local and more accurate name for it is 'Th 'owd brig', which actually dates to the 16th century and was built on an ancient packhorse route at Higherford. This has been carefully restored and is now only open to foot passengers. In a more leisurely age it was an important thoroughfare which is why John Wesley preached from it in 1775.

Barrowford itself is split in two by Pendle Water which is overlooked by the Pendle Heritage Centre. This was, from the 15th century, the home of the Bannister family. Most were yeoman farmers, but one has an honoured place in the world of sport. Sir Roger Bannister was the first man to run a sub-four minute mile.

I always travel in a much more leisurely fashion, as Barrowford is within walking distance of the little town of Colne. One would have thought that this was set too high on a hill to have an aquatic connection, but it does have one sad reminder of the dangers of water.

In this case the water was frozen in the form of an iceberg. On 15th April 1912 the 'unsinkable' *Titanic* was destroyed on her maiden voyage with the loss of 1,490 lives. On Albert Road there is a memorial (*inset*) to Wallace Hartley, the Colne-born musician who was the bandmaster on board the ill-fated ship. As the *Titanic* slipped beneath the waves it was the defiant Wallace Hartley who struck up the tune of the hymn *Nearer My God to Thee*. This to me sounds like a typical example of Lancastrian defiance!

Wycoller

'The sun has set, and the long grass now
Waves dreamily in the evening wind'
Emily Bronte (1818–1848)

When I first knew Wycoller in the 1950s it was a deserted hamlet and one last wonderful reminder of the days when handloom weavers plied their trade from their farms and working cottages. Now the village is the focal point of a country park and the old packhorse trails and ancient bridges link clearly marked footpaths.

Most historians are of the opinion that English villages had their origins between the 9th and 12th centuries. Many of these tiny settlements disappeared from the 14th century onwards as monastic sheep farming swept away hamlets and focused the woollen industry closer to the large abbeys and churches.

Some hamlets, Wycoller included, survived and its name comes from the Anglo-Saxon 'Wic-Air' meaning a dairy farm set among the alder trees. The production of beef and milk as well as mutton and wool was the hamlet's equivalent of our supermarket.

No settlement could have evolved without a reliable source of water and Wycoller beck is an unpolluted joy. The old ford is still there and so are a series of fascinating bridges. The old clapper bridge is composed of a slab of gritstone worn smooth by the feet of generations of handloom weavers. Further upstream is an even more ancient clam bridge also made of a single slab of gritstone and which is one of the oldest in England. It could date to the Bronze Age.

It is the hump-backed bridge shown opposite, however, which attracts the visitors. This was a motorway bridge of its age with hundreds of packhorses passing over the span each day en route from Colne or to Haworth and onwards to the wool market in Halifax.

Wycoller Hall (*inset*) is one of the most famous places in English literature because Charlotte Bronte used it as the inspiration for Mr Rochester's Ferndean Manor in her novel *Jane Eyre*. Wycoller was not deserted when the Bronte sisters walked the footpaths from Haworth. The handloom weavers were then hard at work and packhorses jingled their way over the bridge.

Burnley

`The Man of Wealth and pride
Takes up Space that many poor supplied.'
Oliver Goldsmith, *The Deserted Village* (1770)

Most towns would be glad of one wonderful old house but Burnley, one of the bastions of Old King Cotton's empire, has two. Towneley Hall is a gem of a place situated close to Turf Moor, home of Burnley Football Club. A few miles away is the contrasting manorial pile of Gawthorpe whose extensive parkland is partly owned by the football club as a training ground.

For centuries Towneley Hall (*opposite*) was the home of a family which has its origins around 1200. About this time the Norman Roger de Lacy gave the estate to his son-in-law Geoffrey Towneley who used it as a hunting lodge set within what was then a huge forest. In the mid 1990s the local council, aided by lottery money, created the Forest of Burnley. Today it is busy increasing the tree cover which was devastated from 1500 onwards but sadly accelerated as the Industrial Revolution gathered pace.

During the 16th century the Towneleys were staunch Catholics and their faith over more than two centuries cost them dear. The chapel built for the family around 1500 has an ornate altar piece added by Charles Towneley (1737–1805) who was a famous art collector. His treasures are now located in the British Museum.

The house and its surrounding acres were acquired in 1900 by the Burnley Corporation for the 'perpetual enjoyment of the public'. There is an art gallery and craft museum, whilst the stables overlooking the pond are now converted into a cafe.

In contrast Gawthorpe Hall some five miles away at Padiham (*inset*) was the home of the Shuttleworth family who were as fierce in their Protestant faith as the Towneleys were in sticking to their Catholic beliefs. During the Tudor and Stuart periods the families were obviously at loggerheads, especially during the Civil War.

In the late 1840s Charlotte Bronte visited the Shuttleworths and described Gawthorpe as 'much to my taste, near three centuries old, grey stately and picturesque'.

I was lucky enough to meet the equally stately Miss Rachael Kay-Shuttleworth, the last of the line to live at Gawthorpe. After her death, the house and her fine collection of embroidery were donated to the National Trust in the 1970s.

Burnley and Accrington Markets

'When a newly founded town or borough of the 13th and 14th centuries acquired under its charter the right to hold weekly markets, it needed a space for the market and then a market cross at its focal point … Geoffrey Grigson (1966).

Burnley obtained its first market charter in 1293 and no doubt the place was a busy meeting place in medieval times, being situated close to St Peter's church which dates back at least to 1122.

The old market cross is still situated close to the church in the grounds of the Old Grammar School along with the town well, but today the market area is a modern bustling complex (*opposite*) which looks like many others dating to the 1960s. There are those who still remember the majestic Victorian market hall where the mouth watering pie and black peas, beef and cowheel and UCP tripe and onions attracted hungry queues.

Burnley's market days, Monday, Thursday and

Saturday, are certainly worth visiting on but those who also want to wallow in the past but still shop in the present should journey the six miles to Accrington's market hall which is busy on a Tuesday.

Accrington's market hall (*inset*) with its roof of cast iron and glass is an architectural gem with its busy narrow galleries all reached through a Roman style entrance built in 1868. Accrington is proud of its market hall and also of its annual food fair held in the spring. The town crier never fails to mention that the town will keep faith with its old building and he also points out that in the 1960s other towns destroyed their industrial heritage.

Accrington's name translates as 'the settlement where oak trees grow'. This obviously relates to the fruit of the oak, which is the acorn and London's Acton has the same origin. It is possible to buy a leaflet at the Tourist Information Centre called the Acorn Trail. This traces the history of the area from the days of the prehistoric oak forest to the present time.

The Town Hall is a memorial to Robert Peel whose family moved to Bury from Accrington. The Haworth art gallery has the finest collection of Tiffany glass outside the United States, and the town was the home of the first Ewbank carpet sweeper!

It is the contrast of the old Accrington market hall with the modern structure at Burnley which deserves to link the towns firmly into the Tourist Trail.

Ribchester

'From Penigent's proud foot from my source I slide,
That mountain my proud sire ...'
Michael Drayton (1563–1631), *Polyolbion*

Michael Drayton's description of the birth of the River Ribble encompasses the sentiment to perfection. The three peaks of Whernside, Penyghent and Ingleborough are over 2,000 ft and so qualify as mountains. Pendle falls short of this designation by a mere 169 ft. From the banks of the Ribble at Ribchester (*opposite*) the whale-like outline of Pendle can clearly be seen.

On the Ribble catchment there are some truly wonderful villages typical of the glories of North Western England. The most historic, however, has to be Romantic Ribchester which looks a treat on any day of the year.

Ribchester is one of the most important Roman sites in Northern Britain. The Roman museum set on the banks of the river was purpose built in 1914. Thankfully a recent lottery grant has enabled an extension to be built and the thousands of exhibits are graphically displayed. Here can be found pottery, coinage, leather and stone artefacts.

Since the Romans were in residence between the 2nd and 5th centuries the Ribble has changed course and engulfed sections of the fort, which was originally shaped like a playing card with a tower at each corner. Much of the stonework is incorporated within the structure of the church of St Wilfrid which dates mainly to the 13th century. St Wilfrid was Archbishop of York in the 7th century which seems to suggest that Christianity came early to Ribchester.

Just to underline that cleanliness is next to godliness a short walk along the river from the museum leads to the old Roman bathhouse (*inset*) which has been restored in recent years as have the very substantial granaries. Many ask why the granaries were so extensive? Ribchester was home to more than 500 cavalry and servicing such a large enterprise must have meant that Bremetannacum Veteranorum, as Ribchester was once called, was one of the busiest places in Roman England.

From its foundation in AD 80 until well into the 5th century soldier veterans with 25 or more years' service were given local land on which to settle. Thus there is many a pint of Roman blood still flowing in East Lancashire veins.

Clitheroe

*'Good old Pendle. How oft in youth thy summit we have climbed …
And viewed anon the smiling landscape rich and rare.'*
Harrison Ainsworth (1805–1882), *The Lancashire Witches.*

Clitheroe's town charter was granted in 1147 and it is thus the second oldest borough in Lancashire, beaten only by Wigan. Although a new market complex has been recently completed, the architect has preserved the feel of a medieval market place. It is based in an open-air complex of buildings entered through an archway.

Solidly perched on top of Castle Hill is the Norman keep with walls around 9 ft thick and dating to the 11th century. Clitheroe was one of the castles which Cromwell 'knocked about a bit' during the Civil War. The views of the town from the castle battlements (*opposite*) are, to say the least, panoramic and dominated by Pendle. Part of the castle complex now houses a compact museum devoted to the history of the Ribble valley and its limestone scenery. Clitheroe has long been famous for its quarrying industry which is still a major employer in the area.

Old quarry workings have now been developed into a riverside walk featuring an increasingly popular sculpture trail (*inset*). This is situated along a scenic section of the Ribble Way long distance footpath between Brungerley Bridge and West Bradford on the road between Waddington and Clitheroe.

The sculpture trail has allowed local artists full reign but this is also an area where a very talented lady with a lot of experience in environmental art paints her own tapestry. She is Mother Nature and along this stretch of the Ribble Way she has sown the seeds of rare plants such as white butterbur and bee orchid, blended with common flowers such as thyme and tutsan, harebell and honeysuckle, violet and valerian, bugle and bluebell plus a tangled jungle of other joys.

Clitheroe and the countryside have been comfortable companions throughout the centuries.

Pendle Hill and Downham

'Off on Pendle's side one hears
A passing sound of distant bells …'
Dr Whittaker, *Handbook of Whalley* (1780).

Pendle is an infamous hill because of the witchcraft trials of 1612 and this has led to writers resorting to such statements as 'brooding', 'scowling' and 'evil secrets hidden in a cowl of mist'. I prefer to leave the witchcraft to those who like the macabre and to me the glorious hill (*opposite*) is a symphony of sacred sound with a blend of curlew, snipe, lapwing, grouse and skylark punctuated by the constant chatter of little brooks chuckling their way from the summit.

On the side of the hill are several attractive villages which make the choice of a favourite very difficult. To most people, however, Downham would be high on the list and those who love black and white classic films will know that *Whistle Down the Wind* starring a young Hayley Mills was filmed here and would still recognise several locations.

Visit Downham in the springtime and the daffodils will add an extra dimension to the scene (*inset*). Visit the place on a Sunday morning and you will hear the churchbells tolling. Inside the church is a bell once belonging to Whalley Abbey, which is within walking distance of Downham. Some describe Downham as a feudal village but it is much more friendly and cosy than that. Here reside the Assheton family who have been present for upwards of 600 years and who still look after the estate with conservation always at the forefront of their minds.

Visit the village on a winter's evening and from the lights of the Assheton Arms watch the wood smoke curling upwards from the cottage chimneys. My lasting memory of Downham will always be the smell of burning wood mingling with the aroma of beef roasting in the hotel kitchens, with snowflakes drifting on the chill of the wind.

Preston

'And now I'm here set down again in peace
After my troubles, business, voyages …'
Charles Cotton (1630–1687), *Epistle to John Bradshaw.*

These days it is difficult to imagine Preston as a thriving port with businessmen travelling the world but this was indeed the case until almost the end of the 1970s. All that now remains is the neatly designed and increasingly popular marina (*opposite*) catering for leisure rather than commercial mariners.

But what of the wonderful old town itself? Lancaster has never been pleased that Preston is recognised as the administrative centre of the county, declaring that Preston is only a young upstart.

How can this be true of a town whose Guild has survived since 1328 when its Merchants Court was granted by Henry II? Members of the Guild were bound

on pain of fine and having their trading rights revoked to deal honestly with all customers. At first the meeting of the Guild was an annual event but from 1542 onwards it has been held every 20 years with the only interruptions being during the upheavals of the First and Second World Wars. These days the original function of fair play has been taken over by the Trades Descriptions Act and the Guild is now only a wonderful excuse for the town to hold impressive celebrations.

Preston (or Priests Town) has never been short of religious houses, all set close to the highest navigable point on the River Ribble. Market charters (in addition to the Guild) go back to 1100. The names of the streets read like an historical text book – look out for Friargate and Fishergate which tell of monks and good food. The two have always gone together it would seem.

The Harris Museum and Art Gallery is just one of the magnificent Victorian and Georgian buildings (*inset*) which make the name of Proud Preston an accurate one. Harris was a rich clergyman whose will provided the means to construct this classical neo-Greek-style masterpiece which was built in 1893.

Some have compared the Harris to the British Museum but to the folk of Preston the Harris is the product of the town's unique history. We must never forget the architecture and the ships which once sailed the world and the cotton which made fortunes for many local folk.

Hoghton Tower

'Second Course: Quails, poults, herons, plovers, chickens, pear tart, rabbit, pease buttered, ducks, gammon of bacon, red deer pye, pigeons, wild boar pie, curlews, dry neat's tongue, neat's tongue tart, dried hogs cheek.'
Sunday night's supper for James I at Hoghton Tower, August 1617.

The term *neat* in the 17th century meant an ox. Just think that this was only the second course of supper; and the King had already been given a 'huge lunch'. No wonder the de Hoghton family almost went bankrupt during the three day gargantuan feast.

I love talking to Sir Bernard de Hoghton whose ancestors arrived in England as part of William of Normandy's famous victory at Hastings. He is a fierce advocate, insisting on continual efforts to improve the water quality of the River Darwen which meanders around the tower.

The present tower is a photographer's delight. It was built in 1565 by Thomas de Hoghton, but some alterations were made in the 19th century to provide the comforts required in a family house of this period.

Until recent years the idea of William Shakespeare having Lancashire connections was regarded with either scepticism, humour or a combination of both.

There is now irrefutable evidence indicating that as a young man whose family were Catholic and not welcome in Warwickshire, he was sent to Lancashire. He lived at Hoghton Tower for almost a year and it was here and in other Catholic houses in Lancashire that he sang, acted and began to write plays.

So look carefully at Hoghton Tower and in addition to soaking up the atmosphere of the stones, think of Will Shakespeare and also of the feast of James I. Here there is a huge table at which the King sat. It was here that he looked at a succulent joint of beef and said, 'Arise Sir Loin.'

The local pub is now called the Sirloin and although the menu is impressive it bears no resemblance to the feast at the de Hoghtons' Tower in August of the year 1617!

Lytham

'O' Windmill Land, dear Windmill Land
May thy white towers for ever stand'
Allen Clarke (1863–1935)

Whilst Lytham's is Lancashire's most famous windmill there are others, especially on the Fylde, which are wonderful memories of a bygone and much more tranquil age.

Most local folk, including the present writer, still occasionally object to the joint name of Lytham St Annes. Until 1923 the two settlements were entirely separated – indeed St Annes was once nothing more than a small chapel of ease.

Lytham, which is set proudly on the banks of the Ribble estuary, has an ancient lineage. There has been a long tradition of ship building here and during the 19th century the boat yards were a hive of activity. One of the most famous vessels built here saw valiant service as 'The African Queen', in the movie starring Humphrey Bogart and Katherine Hepburn.

Even as late as the Second World War the Lytham yards were making history – here were constructed, in great secrecy, sections of the Mulberry harbours prior to being transported to the Normandy beaches.

Some of the finest links golf courses in the world are found on the Lancashire coast and the Lytham course (*opposite*) is one of several on the rota to host the Open Championship.

The town itself is a joy and stretches more than a mile between the promenade and the central beach. The windmill (*inset*) was built in Trafalgar year (1805) and has had more than its share of fire and tempest damage but there is always a ground swell of local opinion which, thankfully, insists on restoration.

The mill and the old lifeboat station incorporate a museum which charts the brave deeds of the crews. The most famous disaster was the wreck of the steamship *Mexico* in 1885 which cost the lives of 27 crewmen from the lifeboats of Lytham and of Southport, on the opposite bank of the sweeping bird-rich estuary of the Ribble.

St Annes

'Some rules must be formed … to prevent men bathers shamefully exposing their persons to the great annoyance of females …' P. Whittle (July 1824)

Whilst Lytham's history goes back to Domesday and it had a Benedictine Abbey associated with the mother monastery at Durham until the 1530s, St Annes is but an infant.

The posh people of 'leafy Lytham' looked askance at Blackpool and called it vulgar. Despite this they envied its income and the area around St Anne's chapel was designed as an up-market resort.

The opening up of the railway network, from the 1850s onwards, allowed the rich men in the cotton trade to build impressive residences overlooking the sea. They could easily commute from Lytham and St Annes to 'Cottonopolis'. Their majestic houses still stand.

St Annes pier (*opposite*) was opened by Lord Stanley in 1885 and is a fine building. Pier construction has been a uniquely British institution and each and every one must be preserved. The mock-Tudor entrance to St Annes pier gives the impression of a much greater age. Pier entertainment at St Annes in Victorian and Edwardian times was of a high standard. The large hotels also competed for custom and the great orchestras, including Geraldo's, were regular visitors until the outbreak of the Second World War.

If you are in search of elegant buildings then why not stroll along St Anne's Road West. There are impressive stone pillars and gracefully arched windows over Booths supermarket. The HSBC bank is another grand building, whilst the former Lloyds bank has a set of splendid leaded windows. This grade II listed building is now the base of the Lytham Heritage Group.

The Victorians loved gardens and Lytham St Annes has its share of colourful and beautifully designed parks with my favourite being Ashton Gardens (*inset*). Artist Maggie Howarth has painstakingly put together an open air mosaic which is in perfect keeping with the historical and architectural elegance of the twin settlements.

A stroll around Maggie's Mosaic will reveal a potted pictorial history of Lytham and St Annes, now at last working together to celebrate their contrasting ancient and modern cultures.

Blackpool Tower and Wrea Green

Give us, Lord
A bit o' sun
A bit o' wark
An' a bit of fun
Allen Clarke (1897)

Having lived in Blackpool part of my life I despair when I hear the town described as only Brash, Breezy and Boozy. Blackpool has for more than 150 years provided tourists with whatever they wanted including access to stretches of attractive countryside.

There has been a settlement around Wrea Green (*inset*) certainly since the 12th century and perhaps even earlier with many historians suggesting an Anglo-Saxon origin.

Until the 19th century the village was known only as 'Wray' which comes from the Danish word Vra meaning a secluded corner. In 1860 the postal service began to develop assisted by the railway network and confusion

was caused due to the fact that there was also a Wray near Lancaster.

The Fylde name was, therefore, changed to Wrea Green and what a joy it is to sit by the large village pond and watch cricket being played on the green. The sound of bird song mingled with the thud of leather ball on willow bat suggests that Wrea Green has been untouched by industry. In the 19th century, however, there was a huge brickworks in the centre of the village with the essential clay being gouged out of what is now the pond. Environmental work in the 1980s has produced an ecological miracle and all this within a 20 minute drive of Blackpool Tower.

Always determined to stay one step ahead of the field in the annals of tourism, Blackpool erected its 518 ft tower (*opposite*) in 1894. Until the construction of London's Post Office Tower, more than 80 years later, Blackpool boasted the highest building in Britain.

The legs of Blackpool's tower straddle an ornate ballroom with its famous Wurlitzer organ, bars and restaurants. It also has an aquarium, a zoo and even an Education Heritage Museum. The latter came too late to educate Stanley Holloway's young Albert Ramsbottom who visited the mythical lion called Wallace, poked him in the ear with a stick with a horse's head handle and 'got et'.

Blackpool Illuminations

'Holidaymakers first tripped the light fantastic in Blackpool in 1879 when just eight
arc lamps bathed the promenade in what was described as artificial sunshine.'
Tourism Services Department, *A History of Blackpool Illuminations*, 1995

My own memories of the illuminations go back to the early 1950s when a relative had a garage on the outskirts of Blackpool. I earned money whilst a student by serving petrol and I now live close to that garage. From my bedroom window I have a clear view of the tower and during the autumn of the illuminations.

It all began seriously in 1897 when five illuminated tramcars rattled their way up and down the promenade. It seems that the idea evolved as a result of Berlin's celebrations to mark the Kaiser's birthday.

By 1912 the idea had gained support and at that time the resort's 'decorative lighting' produced an influx of visitors during the autumn. Steam train excursions came from the cotton towns of Lancashire.

The First World War snuffed out the lights and it was only in 1923 that a spectacular festival resurrected the tradition. Obviously the second war with Germany disrupted the evolution and the lights were only switched on again in 1949.

I was present at the 1949 switch on and for most years since. Blackpool has always been a resort not just to keep up with rivals but to keep one step ahead. The illuminations' engineers still switch on more than half a million bulbs of many colours but to these are added all the modern laser and electronic technology – a wonderful mix between the old and the new.

The same is true of the tramcars (*inset*) which have been a feature of the resort since July 1898. Other towns and cities in Britain are now realising that Blackpool was right not to abandon its tram system and the rattle and rumble of this environmentally efficient transport is now reappearing in other towns and cities, including Manchester.

Poulton-le-Fylde and Skippool

'How many thousands of these trees now stand
Black, broken on their rootes …'
Richard James (1592–1638), *Iter Lancastre (Lancastrian Journey)*

At one time the whole of what is now Lancashire was a vast forest running from the hills to the fringes of the sea. From the Bronze Age onwards the tree cover has been stripped without a thought for conservation.

In some cases climatic changes have not helped natural recovery and just off the coast are the remains of an ancient and long submerged forest. From the 17th century onwards demand for trees outstripped supply. Many harbours came into being because of the import of timber especially from Russia. This was certainly the case with Wardleys Creek and Skippool (*inset*) which are now tiny inlets on opposite banks of the Wyre. Both are popular with pleasure craft but their glory days have long gone along with the days of sail. From Skippool Creek a well marked footpath leads to Stannah where there is a visitor and ecology centre, with weather-proofed panels giving details of the rich history of the Wyre estuary.

Both ports, during the 17th to 19th centuries, were controlled from the grand little market town of Poulton-le-Fylde. I remember the glare of publicity which beamed down on this area in 1970 when the bones of an elk were discovered at nearby Carlton. The spear points of the hunters on the look out for protein around 10,000 BC were still embedded in the bones.

Poulton, meaning the town by the pool, is steeped in history (*opposite*) and here are stone stocks, a 17th-century whipping post and a set of fish stones. These stand on one side of the pedestrianised town centre with the church of St Chad dominating the other.

There is mention of a church in 1094 but there was almost certainly a Christian settlement prior to the Conquest. The church has been restructured several times and the Georgian interior is worth travelling miles to see. So are the memorials of the Fleetwood-Hesketh family, one of whom – Sir Peter – built the modern town of Fleetwood during the 1840s.

Lancastrians make a pilgrimage to the church in spring when the area is surrounded by colourful swathes of crocus, some of which almost conceal the grave of Edward Sherdley. He made the mistake of having the skull and crossbones carved on his headstone and he has ever since been branded a pirate.

St Michael's on Wyre

'Dear water, clear water, playful in all your streams …
Pure being, perfect in music and movement?'
W.H. Auden (1907–1973)

In the early days the banks above the shallow areas of rivers were the obvious places to build settlements. Two of the most beautiful fords along the course of the River Wyre are at St Michael's (*opposite*) and at the obviously named Cartford. These fords have survived the ravages of time and would still be recognised by those living more than a century ago.

Cartford is the only remaining toll bridge over the Wyre (*inset*) and beyond this is Wild Boar Cottage. Incorporated into this is one of the large carriages from the Big Wheel which dominated Blackpool until it was demolished in 1928.

Until recently there was a second and much larger toll bridge over the Wyre. This was at Shard, a word which is

old Norse and means 'shallows'. The modern bridge is not tolled but at the Shard Bridge Hotel the old bridge supports can still be seen and many artefacts of the old span are on display inside and outside the hostelry.

St Michael's is a delightful time warp of a village dominated by the church from which it takes its name. This was founded as early as AD 640 and set close to the ancient ford which is now obviously bridged.

At the eastern end of the church is a sundial bearing the inscription, 'Our days upon earth are as a shadow'. A careful examination of the base would seem to prove the suggestion that here is the support of an old Saxon preaching cross. The religious settlement here was probably founded by followers of Paulinus in the 7th century.

Recent engineering to prevent flooding has meant that St Michael's is now very much 'on' as opposed to 'in' the Wyre which was not always the case in the past!

The church has many features dating from the 13th and 14th centuries, including the famous 'lepers' squint', a window through which those with contagious diseases could watch services without infecting the congregation.

One of the highlights of any visit to St Michael's should be to walk along the footpath from which there are splendid views of the meandering loop of the Wyre, which seems to snuggle the historic church in a warm embrace.

Crook of Lune and Calder Vale

'On each side rise two sloping hills … between them in the richest valleys the Lune
serpentines for many a mile and comes forth ample and clear.'
Thomas Gray (1716–1771)

Two of Lancashire's most beautiful rivers are the Lune (*opposite*) and the Wyre, both of which have fast flowing and twisting tributaries. Although neither of these rivers was blighted by the machinations of the Industrial Revolution, both the Wyre and Lune demonstrate how the textile industry had its origins because of the power of water.

Nowhere is this point better illustrated than at Calder Vale (*inset*), which is reached via narrow roads and long winding footpaths leading through woodlands.

Calder Vale was purpose built in 1835 by the Quakers Richard and Jonathan Jackson who wished to combine philanthropy with profits for themselves. The village complex is still there with the large four-storeyed Lappet Mill, the Long Row of workers' terraced dwellings, the school, and also remaining are the mill race and feeder ponds for Low Mill. The latter is now only a ruin. Calder House, the Jackson family home, is now a restaurant and a pleasant spot to satisfy both a gastronomic and an historical appetite.

Calder Vale village is atmospheric rather than just scenically beautiful and therefore a very real contrast to the views from the footpaths leading from the Crook of Lune car park.

Thomas Gray was one of Britain's most renowned landscape poets and his opinion of this area was confirmed by the artist J.M.W. Turner (1775–1851) who spent many

hours capturing the serpentine twistings of the Crook of Lune on his canvasses. These days the car park is sandwiched between a new road and an old railway bridge. The latter once linked Lancaster's Green Ayre station to Wennington but in 1966 this fell victim to the Beeching closures. The track was lifted and the route has now been developed into an attractive nature reserve.

Both Gray and Turner would have appreciated the views from the railway bridge. There is always wildlife to be seen and there are interpretation boards to identify the various species whilst other boards explain the history of the railway and the industries which once operated within the valley.

Slaidburn and the River Hodder

'A great bed of rushes on the fell top conserves the water and gives birth to the river. From rushes dripping over the peat-hag, water drips unceasingly dimpling the blackness below. And so the Hodder is born.' Jessica Lofthouse (1946).

Does the name Slaidburn refer to a battle stone by the River Hodder which was once a memorial to the Anglo-Saxons who fell in battle against the Danes? Or could the name mean a sheep enclosure close to the river? There are terraced fields called lychets near the grand old church, thus indicating an Anglo-Saxon settlement. Whatever the correct interpretation might be, I love the ambience of Slaidburn and the glorious countryside (*opposite*) which surrounds it.

There are still some wonderful places to be explored along the Hodder catchment. Between Slaidburn and the Cross of Greet (*inset*) is Stocks Reservoir. This takes its name from the village which was submerged during the 1930s to create a reservoir supplying drinking water for the developing Fylde coast resorts.

When Stocks was flooded some of the stones from the church were removed at the villagers' insistence and a new church was built alongside the road. Inside this there are photographs and newspaper articles depicting the story of the flooding.

Bowland is Nature's Kingdom and Slaidburn was once the focal point of a large and prosperous farming community. Look out for the bridge over the Hodder, explore the charming church with its 17th-century three-decker pulpit and note the grammar school dated 1717 but which now forms part of the modern day primary school.

Many come to enjoy a meal in the oak beamed lounge of the Hark to Bounty Inn, said to take its name from a 19th-century landowner. Waiting outside one day was the pack of hounds and when the leader barked his master said, 'Hark to Bounty'. The name was instantly adopted and the much more mundane name of 'The Dog' disappeared into history.

Upstairs at the inn is the 19th-century courthouse complete with bench, bar and a place for the jury and observers. A request to see this piece of Hodder history is not denied to present day visitors.

The Trough of Bowland

'Full many a glorious morning have I seen'
Shakespeare, *Sonnets* (1595)

Standing on the 1,000 ft summit of the Trough of Bowland is my idea of heaven. A raindrop falling on the carpet of moss is eventually squeezed down a valley to join the River Hodder near Dunsop Bridge. Another drop of rain only a foot away will become part of the flow of the River Wyre which eventually reaches the sea at Fleetwood.

The moss itself mainly consists of sphagnum which used to be called 'battle grass'. It was used until the end of the First World War to pack wounds. Research has shown that the moss contains compounds which not only help blood to clot but which also contain an antiseptic. It would seem that battle grass was more use than a grubby bandage!

There is a wonderful swirl of water when the Marshaw Wyre joins the Tarnbrook Wyre near Abbeystead (*inset*). As the name implies there was once an abbey farm here and the 13th-century Cistercians planned a large monastery but the winter climate proved too severe.

If ever evidence was needed to prove that Lancashire is not merely an industrial county then the Trough of Bowland (*opposite*) provides it. The ancient highway, marked by finger posts and milestones, still links Clitheroe with Lancaster.

Here are farms mainly concentrating upon sheep but many are now diversifying and provide excellent bed and breakfast accommodation. Some offer, for sale, fresh eggs, jars of jam and especially honey. Here the aroma of Bowland heather is yours for the asking and delivered almost directly from the hive.

At one time it was very difficult to walk around the Trough of Bowland but modern day landowners now allow access to most wild places. Strolling is therefore much easier and the footpaths are well marked. North West Water are very imaginative in developing compromises between catchment and countryside access.

Here are the haunts of hen harrier, curlew, red grouse, redshank and skylark. Wild Lancashire is indeed a wonderful place to enjoy sunshine, snow flakes or showers.

Halton and the Lune

'There are much nicer counties – or so people say,
But have they walked along Pendle's Green Way?
Or seen the wild geese winging over the Lune?
Or climbed Winter Hill by the light of the Moon?
Benita Moore (1995)

A selection of images to record the Lune and the Trough of Bowland is not easy. The whole area is so beautiful that those who do not know Lancashire cannot imagine what the county has on offer to the landscape photographer or the artist.

The village of Halton (*opposite*) is set away from the main road and it is difficult to realise that in Saxon times this settlement was more important than Lancaster. Prior to 1066 it was the power base of Earl Tostig, the warrior brother of King Harold. In 1066 the two estranged brothers met in battle at Stamford Bridge near York. Tostig was killed and Harold's victorious but tired army had then to march south in a hurry in order to confront the invading William of Normandy and, not surprisingly, was defeated near Hastings.

From the church look up to the hill and you will see the flat-topped castle mound where Tostig had his wooden fortification.

The church is dedicated to St Wilfrid, the 7th-century cleric and in the churchyard is an attractive cross (*inset*) which has a fascinating mix of Christian and pagan symbols. This shows that early Christians were almost, but not quite, sure that the new religion had replaced the pagan beliefs.

Lancaster

'Let him that is no coward nor no flatterer …
Pluck a red rose from off this thorn with me'
Shakespeare (1564–1616), *Henry IV Part 1 (Act 2 Scene 4)*

No portrait of Lancashire could ever be complete without reference to the red rose which symbolises our county. Obviously the spectacularly scenic settlement of Lancaster is the place to discover the emblem of England.

The defiant words penned by Shakespeare on behalf of the character John Beaufort in *Henry IV*, have echoed across time as a 15th-century bloodthirsty quarrel between the houses of York and Lancaster. The red rose (*Rosa officinalis*) is still the symbol for Lancashire but the rose of England is now the Tudor rose. The death of Richard III at Bosworth in Leicestershire in 1483 led to the establishment of the Tudor dynasty. The first Tudor (Henry VII) had the blood of both the house of Lancaster and York in his veins and at that time the English (or Tudor) rose was symbolically reconstructed of red and white portions.

But what of Lancaster itself? Here is not one but two millennia of historic events with a splendid Norman castle built on top of the Roman Lune Caster. This in turn was perched atop an Iron Age settlement with the River Lune curling around the settlement like a contented dog.

The castle (*opposite*), part of which still serves as a court of law and a prison, has history carved in each and every stone with the most impressive structure being the 14th-century Gatehouse attributed to the first Duke of Lancaster, John of Gaunt.

Lancaster survived the Industrial Revolution almost, but not quite unscathed. Here were a few cotton mills and other factories specialising in the production of linoleum which was also known as oil cloth. In the 18th century until the Lune silted up Lancaster was a prosperous port.

The views of and from Williamson Park and memorial are dramatic. In 1878 Alderman James Williamson had made a fortune from linoleum and so had his father before him, the latter becoming Lord Ashton. The 38 acre Williamson Park is dominated by a Portland stone memorial to James' wife (*inset*). The park was landscaped from an old quarry and the copper domed building has viewing balconies and displays depicting local history.

Morecambe and Heysham

*'The Gravesend of Lancaster. It is much frequented by the trippers from the busy
towns of Lancashire …'* Town advertisement of the 1870s.

Until very recently it has seemed that Morecambe had something of an identity crisis. Should it copy Blackpool and become big, brash and benefiting from an influx of brass? Or should it follow Southport and become posh and attract a more up market clientele?

In the event it did neither and it was only in the 1990s that the resort found its own niche – this is to market an irresistible combination of history and natural history.

The resort has at last learned to appreciate the value of its wonderful bird-rich bay, with the Lake District mountains as a backdrop. Ornithologists now travel miles to visit Morecambe Bay and the town's most famous birdwatcher was Eric Bartholomew. He is best known to

the world as Eric Morecambe. Eric loved the town and its wildlife and he also made a song famous: *Bring me Sunshine.*

Morecambe is a beautiful spot even in the rain and the Tern Project based around the stone jetty (*opposite*) is a place for all seasons. It has developed into an open air sculpture park which accurately portrays the birds which are to be found around the Bay.

Morecambe was named after the Bay as tourists began to arrive. A map of 1848 shows four settlements, namely Poulton-le-Sands, Torrisholme, Bare and Heysham, the latter having the longest and most distinguished history.

St Peter's church at Heysham is now mainly 14th-century but its foundation dates back to the 8th century. Beyond St Peter's a delightfully attractive path, now in the care of the National Trust but freely accessible, leads up to the ruins of what is considered to be Lancashire's oldest church.

The Chapel of St Patrick (*inset*) is perched on an outcrop of sandstone. Even in its heyday it was less than 30 ft long and 10 ft wide and was used by Irish based Christians who sailed into the Bay between the 6th and 8th centuries.

The soil around the chapel is so thin that graves were hewn out of solid rock and there they remain to the present time. It was probably due to the Viking raids that the chapel was abandoned and replaced by St Peter's church which has a more sheltered location.

The Kent Estuary at Arnside

'… a brave River where the famous cockles of old England is gathered in the sands scraped out with hookes like sickles …' Sandford, *Antiquities and Familyes* (1675).

This account of catching cockles and flat fish reminds me of my early life in the Furness district along the then Lancashire and Cumberland border just after the Second World War. In 1974 this district was re-organised into the new county of Cumbria. I remember these marine riches of Morecambe Bay but Bill Meadows' picture of the Kent Estuary Bore at Arnside (*inset*) is a reminder of the fact that the dangerous tide can come in here at a rate equalling that of a galloping horse. The peace of the Arnside boats at anchor (*opposite*) is in sharp contrast to the dangers associated with the Bore which, on a spring tide, can be as awe inspiring as that of the more famous Severn.

Arnside is surrounded by wonderful walking country but this is not an area in which to stride out quickly but

rather to stroll slowly in order to soak up the atmosphere. The walk up to the summit of the Arnside Knott, a limestone outcrop, is a botanist's paradise in summer whilst in the colder months of the year the flocks of wildfowl and waders around the bay are always interesting and occasionally spectacular.

Fortunately the Knott is owned by the National Trust and is therefore now safe from development. A knott is an old name for a bunch of flowers. Thus the phrase 'here we go gathering knotts in May' makes more sense than the more traditional word 'nuts'.

The Kent is said to be the fastest flowing river in England and it crashes down from the High Street mountains above Kendal before reaching the sea at Arnside. This is a pretty little spot which became a popular, if small, seaside resort following the construction of the Furness Railway in the 1850s.

The effect of the Kent estuary bore is emphasised as it hurtles through the supports of the railway viaduct. This links Arnside to Grange-over-Sands and is 165 yards long. In its heyday Arnside had a short but profitable period of wooden boat construction and also for an even shorter time there was a small pier from which pleasure steamers plied to and from Fleetwood, Morecambe and Barrow-in-Furness.

Arnside is one of those wonderful places where time does indeed stand still and where, in an increasingly busy world, the words leisure and pleasure are easily linked.

LANCASHIRE
A portrait in colour

Lancashire is a county of broad contrasts. To the south there are the industrial areas of Bolton, Wigan, Bury and Rochdale; to the west there are the great coastal resorts of Southport, Blackpool and Morecambe and the fertile Fylde plain; to the east are Clitheroe, Burnley and the hill farming communities of the Pennines; to the north are Lancaster and the moorland villages; and, at the centre, the beautiful Forest of Bowland.

Lancashire is very much a county to explore and enjoy. There are wonderful places to visit at all times of the year and reminders of famous events, and of historical and literary figures from its past are everywhere.

In his evocative photographs, Bill Meadows seeks to reflect the county in all its moods and colours from the regeneration of the old cotton mills and docksides to the flourishing cities and countryside of modern Lancashire.

The text by local broadcaster and journalist, Ron Freethy, a native of Lancashire chronicles the county's historic past and demonstrates just how much it has to offer today, both to local people and visitors alike.

Bill Meadows became fascinated by landscape photography at an early age. As a teenager he experimented with an old folding Kodak camera and made countless sorties into the countryside to capture the changing face of nature within it. He is now a leading photographer whose work is increasingly requested for use in a wide variety of publications. He has built up a huge archive of images and continues to accept commissions for new books in this photographic series on the English counties. Four volumes already completed by Bill include those on *Cheshire*, *Derbyshire*, *Leicestershire & Rutland*, and *Warwickshire*.

Ron Freethy is a well-known Lancashire broadcaster and journalist. He lives near Blackpool with his wife, Marlene, who helps with the research and with the preparation of Ron's numerous radio programmes. Ron has also written many books on local subjects including *Hidden Lancashire* and the recently published *Lancashire Privies*.

Front cover photograph: The Forest of Bowland
Back cover photograph: Morecambe Promenade